Celebrate—
WHILE WE WAIT

Family Devotional Resources for Advent and Christmas Too

THE SCHROEDER FAMILY
Ted, Linda, Christopher, Joel and Mark

Publishing House
St. Louis

Cover Photo: Ted Schroeder

Concordia Publishing House, St. Louis, Missouri
Copyright © 1977 Concordia Publishing House

MANUFACTURED IN THE UNITED STATES OF AMERICA

Library of Congress Cataloging in Publication Data

Main entry under title:

Celebrate while we wait.

    SUMMARY: Devotional readings for each day of Advent with
prayers and suggestions for family-involvement activities.
        1. Advent—Prayer books and devotions—English.
2. Christmas—Prayer books and devotions—English.
3. Family—Prayer books and devotions—English.
[1. Advent—Prayer books and devotions. 2. Christmas—Prayer
books and devotions. 3. Prayer books and devotions] I. Schroeder,
Ted, 1937-
BV40.C43   242'.33   77-8587
ISBN 0-570-03052-8

Contents

Preface for Parents

We want you to celebrate Advent and Christmas in a family way. The play on words is intentional. We're expecting! We're expecting Christmas and the retelling of the birth of Jesus. That's obvious, but that's not all.

Advent reminds us that we are at all times expectant people, people in waiting, people of promise. Our faith is built on God's promises fulfilled and yet to be fulfilled. We are by God's grace pregnant with new life and eternal hope. That means there's something yet worth waiting for—and perhaps we need practice in waiting.

Advent can be that practice in waiting—if we let Advent be Advent, and wait to let Christmas be Christmas. The devotions in this book are designed to help you wait—and wait meaning-fully. They can stand alone as resources for your family's observance of Advent and Christmas. But we'd also like to share some customs our family has learned and lived with while waiting.

Advent and Christmas—Our Family's Way

When we wait for Christmas, we really wait. We don't put up the Christmas tree or other decorations until December 24th (although we make an adventure of acquiring our tree, and we work together in making decorations). We don't sing Christmas hymns and carols before Christmas (although we learn some new ones to be ready). We don't eat "Christmas cookies" and other goodies before Christmas (although we bake and bake and bake . . . and maybe snitch just one for a taste test). But we don't wait empty-handed or empty-hearted. We've filled Advent with its own customs to help us understand and enjoy our waiting.

For years there has been in our family a six-foot log drilled with 28 holes in a row. It's our Advent log, holding a candle for each day of Advent—an expansion of the traditional Advent wreath holding a candle for each week of Advent. The candles themselves provide much symbolism as we start Advent in the darkness of one candlepower and daily see that light increase as we burn additional candles in anticipation of the birth of the Light of the world. The Advent log also prompts us to be diligent and regular with our family devotions. During the rest of the year we often neglect family worship, but during Advent we don't miss. We can't! If we don't light every candle in proper sequence, the pyramid pattern gets ruined and everyone notices. Besides, no one wants to miss his turn at being candle-lighter-and-snuffer.

We do sing during Advent. We discovered already during their toddler years that our boys could learn anything if it were repeated often enough. During Advent devotions they were (and still are, at ages 11, 12, and 13) a captive audience—captivated by the candles on the Advent log. So together we learned, and together we sing many Advent hymns, traditional and folk.

Years ago, as a way of teaching our very young boys more about Jesus our Messiah, I invented Advent cookies—simple sugar cookies cut into the shapes of seven Messianic symbols, one for each day of the week. We talk about the symbols before we eat the cookies. That one cookie per day in place of our usual more elaborate desserts has also become for us a symbolic fasting, emphasizing the penitential nature of the Advent season. (The cookie symbols are studied in the devotions provided in this book for the second week of Advent. A recipe and patterns are also provided so you can, if you like, introduce the cookie custom to your family at that time). It just wouldn't seem like Advent now for us without those cookies.

So we wait and wait and wait. But then, when Christmas comes, we really celebrate Christmas. For 12 days we celebrate Christmas! We agree with our Christian ancestors who established the liturgical calendar that anything worth waiting for all during Advent, and worth celebrating as much as Jesus' birthday is, shouldn't be allowed to fizzle out in 24 hours. So for 12 days we share festive treats and special activities, enjoy Christmas music, keep up the tree and decorations, and exchange gifts.

That's right, we exchange gifts. Everyone receives one gift each day for 12 days. Not every gift is a big expensive item, of course. It may be a candy bar or a pair of socks, or a homemade picture or a paper promise of something to come, but it's a gift to be opened when we gather around the lighted tree in the morning and play our favorite Christmas records before dashing off to school or office.

Obviously, this custom does away with the Santa Claus custom. Everyone knows he doesn't come 12 days in a row. We deliberately wanted to displace Santa Claus for theological and personal reasons. Theologically, Santa Claus—an anonymous stranger who reportedly spies on the little people and delivers gifts as rewards for their good behavior—totally contradicts the very message of Christmas—that our very personal God, out of great love for us, sent His Son as a gift while we were yet sinners (in fact, *because* we are sinners). And personally, we wanted our children to know their presents were gifts from us, given because we love them.

When they grew old enough to ask about Santa Claus, we simply explained that was a game some people play as a way of giving each other gifts, a game we didn't need to play because we had such fun giving gifts ourselves. Our fears that our children might not be able to cope with cultural pressure evaporated when we heard the four-year-old explain to an inquisitive visitor, "We don't need Santa Claus; Mommy and Daddy give us lots of presents." Now we all vie for the privilege of gifting each other and need a sign-up chart to keep track of who's giving something to whom which day, so we don't each end up with 48 gifts.

People visiting our home during those 12 days are always fascinated by unopened gifts under our tree. So we decided to include guests in our custom, too. All year long we stay alert for and collect "manger gifts"—unusual 10—35¢ items we wrap and place in a straw-filled wooden manger near the door and give to anyone who enters our home during the Christmas season (only the *first* visit, for those who regularly come and go). This custom has been great fun and has greatly enriched our understanding of the theology of gifts.

The same fun and enrichment is true of all the Advent/Christmas traditions in our family. Not only have they made Advent and Christmas more meaningful for us, but they have also made us more a family. We share them in the hope that you, too, will be enriched and perhaps be stimulated to try some new family customs of your own making. We're still creating new ones. One of these years we're going to set out our "gift manger" at the beginning of Advent and add a bit of straw to it each day as a sign of our preparing for Jesus' coming at Christmas.

Notes on the Use of This Book

The devotional readings for each day were written and printed in a style intended to be read by elementary-age children and understood by even younger ones. In addition, Bible readings are suggested each day for further study by older children and adults.

A prayer is provided for each day; but be sure to add your own prayer concerns, both joys and needs, as they are contributed by all members of your family.

Music for three songs ("The King of Glory," "God Promised," and "O Come, O Come, Emmanuel") is provided in the back of this book. For other suggested hymns and songs, plus ones of your own choosing, you will need your own supply of hymnals and/or songbooks.

Frequently suggestions are provided for extra family-involvement activities:

The reading for Advent 1 suggests the use of an Advent log or wreath. See Appendix A.

The reading for Advent 2 suggests the making of people-ornaments. See Appendix B.

The readings for Advent 6 and a number of other days suggest the supplementary reading of Arch Books. Arch Books are inexpensive but colorfully illustrated paperback Bible stories for younger children. Arch Books are published by Concordia Publishing House and are available in most religious book stores. For a complete list of Arch Books suggested for use along with this book, see Appendix D. If you plan to give presents throughout the 12 days of Christmas (see Preface for Parents), consider using the correlated Arch Books as gifts on some of those days.

The readings for Advent 8—14 introduce the Advent cookie custom. See the Preface for Parents for explanation; see Appendix C for recipe and patterns. If you choose not to make the cookies (and maybe even if you do), provide some other visual expression of the symbol for each day's reading—e.g., make paper cutouts from the patterns in this book, or find photos or pictures of the symbols, or gather model objects (stuffed toy or ceramic lamb, real house key, bouquet of flowers, etc.).

One important thing to remember is that Advent begins on the fourth Sunday before Christmas and ends with December 24. Therefore the number of days in Advent varies from 22 (when December 25 is a Monday) to 28 (when December 25 is a Sunday). This book provides material for all 28 days. However, the readings for Advent 23—28 are deliberately flexible; omit or combine them as you see fit.

Throughout the book, in fact, you should feel free to pick and choose among—and by all means expand upon—the suggested resources and activities in order to provide a learning and worship experience suitable for your own family. (For instance, ask your pastor on Sunday what hymns he has chosen for the following Sunday, or the next service. Include those hymns in your family devotions, especially to teach them to the younger children who can't read. Help them learn and memorize at least the first stanza so they can participate meaningfully in the worship service. Or—for the same reason—request that your pastor include in the worship service one of the songs you've first learned at home.)

And to God alone be glory!

Advent 1–7

What Are We Waiting for?
An Introduction

What?

Sunday   FIRST DAY OF ADVENT

"WHAT?"

Advent, that's what.

"What's Advent?"

Advent is a word. It means "coming" or "arrival." Do you know what's coming? Do you know who's coming?

Advent is also a name. It's the name given to the season just before Christmas. (That tells you *what's* coming. Does it tell you *who's* coming?)

Advent is also a time. It's a time of waiting. It's four weeks of waiting for Christmas to come. And Advent is a time to think about waiting. It's a time to remember how people thousands of years ago waited and waited and waited for Jesus to be born. (That tells you who's coming.) This book will give us some things to think about, talk about, pray about, and some things to do, while we wait for Christmas.

Many people use an Advent wreath or Advent log to help them wait. The candles on the wreath (one for each week) or log (one for each day) help mark the passing of time. They also remind us that Jesus came to be the Light of the world. He came, and still comes, to light up our lives with His love. We'll learn more about that in the days ahead.

Advent is also a time to think about why Jesus was born. It's a time to remember all the ways we are unfaithful to God. It's a time to think about all we've done wrong—all the things Jesus came to forgive. Remembering our sins and feeling sorry about them is called penitence. And the color violet is a symbol for penitence. That's why the candles on an Advent wreath or log are usually violet.

Because Jesus did come to forgive our sins, we will live with Him forever. Green leaves, especially evergreens, are a good symbol for eternal life. That's why an Advent wreath or log is usually decorated with evergreens.

So that's what Advent is—a time to wait for Christmas, for Jesus' blessing, for new life with Him.

Prayer: Come, Lord Jesus, come. Come into our home. Come into our hearts. Light up our lives with Your love. Amen.

Bible Readings: Isaiah 56:1; 59:19-21

Songs: "The Advent of Our King"
"The King of Glory" (See page 61)

In addition: Do you have an Advent log or wreath? Be sure to review its symbolism and light the first candle.

If you don't have an Advent wreath or log, see Appendix A for suggestions.

What Are We?

Monday   SECOND DAY OF ADVENT

"What are we?"
A family, that's what.
"What's a family?"
A family is a group of people who *(tell your own ideas)* . . .

Advent is a family affair in several ways. Most important of all, Advent reminds us that we are in God's family. As we wait for Christmas we remember how God the Father promised to send His

Son to be our Brother. God kept that promise. By joining our human family, Jesus made it possible for us to be in God's family.

And if Jesus is your Brother and my Brother, and if God is your Father and my Father, then we're all related. We're all in the same family, even people who don't have the same last name or live in the same house. This bigger family of Christians is the church. That's another way Advent is a family affair. As we wait, we're waiting together with our whole church family around the world.

Our own little family here at home is important, too. Is our family a group of people who care about each other, pray for each other, worship together, learn together? Advent is a good time to practice being that kind of family. Then Christmas will not only be an "it's good to be in God's family" celebration. It will also be an "it's good to be in our family" celebration.

Prayer: Come, Brother Jesus, come. Come to our family at home. Come to our church family. Bless us with Your Father's love. Teach us how to love each other. Amen.

Bible Readings: Ephesians 1:3-10; 4:1-6

Songs: "Oh, Blest the House, Whate'er Befall"
"Our Father by Whose Name"
"In My Family"

In addition: To help celebrate that Jesus came for their family and lives in them, some families put themselves and their friends on their Christmas tree. No, they don't sit in the tree or hang from the branches. They make Christmas ornaments from pictures of themselves and their relatives and friends and hang a picture gallery on the tree. If you would like to try this new custom, see Appendix B.

What! Are We Waiting?

Tuesday   THIRD DAY OF ADVENT

"What!—are we waiting! ?"
    Yes, we're waiting.
"But I just can't wait . . . !"

Oh no? Why not? What makes waiting for anything—or anyone—hard to do? Why are we always impatient?

Think about some of the instant things we enjoy: instant Kool-Aid, instant coffee, instant touch-tone "dialing," instant . . . (make your own list).

What are some things for which we must wait, besides Christmas? (Make your own list . . . .) Are any of those things worth waiting for? Why or why not?

God waited a long, long time—hundreds and thousands of years—before He sent Jesus to earth. All the while He waited, His people had to wait too. They had a hard time waiting. Sometimes they were impatient. Sometimes they thought God would never keep His promise.

But they waited, and God did keep His promise. While they waited, they learned a lot about themselves and about God. They also learned how to wait. (We'll be reading more about that in the days ahead.)

Now we're waiting, too. What can we learn about ourselves while we wait? What can we learn about God? What can we learn about waiting? There are some clues in these Bible verses:

I waited patiently for the Lord; He . . . heard my cry. (Psalm 40:1)

Make me to know Your ways, O Lord; teach me your paths. Lead me in truth, and teach me, for You are the God of my salvation; for You I wait all day long. (Psalm 25:4-5)

The Lord is the everlasting God . . . He does not faint or grow weary. . . . They who wait for the Lord shall renew their strength, they shall mount up with wings like eagles, they shall run and not be weary, they shall walk and not faint. (Isaiah 40:28, 31)

Prayer: God, forgive us for being impatient with You. Teach us to wait for Your blessing. Teach us to trust in Your everyday love. Come, Lord Jesus, come. Amen.

Songs: "Come, O Precious Ransom, Come" (vv. 1, 2)
"Lift Up Your Heads, Ye Mighty Gates" (vv. 1, 5)

Bible Readings: Psalm 62; Isaiah 25:6-9; Isaiah 30:18.

In addition: Make or mark a calendar to count down the days to wait until Christmas. Discuss waiting until December 24 to decorate your home for Christmas and enjoy Christmas treats.

What Are We Waiting For?

Wednesday   FOURTH DAY OF ADVENT

"What are we waiting for?"
   Christmas, that's what.
"What's Christmas?"
   Christmas is *(list your own ideas)* . . .

Christmas is a birthday party, a very special birthday party. It's a birthday party for the Son of God, Jesus Himself. But how can we have a birthday party for someone who isn't here?

Let's stop and think about birthday parties. What is it we celebrate? Is it the date we celebrate? No, not really. Is it the fact that someone was born once upon a time? Well, yes, but that's not all. We don't often celebrate the birthday of someone who is dead already. Most of all a birthday party celebrates a person. It celebrates that someone *is,* that someone is *special,* that someone is *here,* with us now.

Jesus still is. He's certainly special. He's the only Savior we have. And He is here with us now. He's here in the hearts and lives of all those who love Him and believe in Him. So we can have a birthday party for Jesus by having a party with each other.

That's one reason we give each other Christmas presents. In a way it's like giving birthday presents to Jesus. The gifts also remind us of the great gift God gave us when He sent Jesus to live and die and rise again for us.

As we wait for Christmas let's remember what we're waiting for. We're waiting to give a party for Jesus, not get a party for ourselves. We're waiting to celebrate once more God's most special gift to us—His Son, our Savior.

Prayer: Thank You, God, for sending Jesus to be our Savior. Thank You for giving us time to celebrate His birthday. Be in our hearts and bless us. Help us to be good gifts to each other. Amen.

Bible Readings: Matthew 25:31-40; Colossians 3:14-17

Songs: "To Thee My Heart I Offer" (vv. 1, 5)
"The King of Glory" (See page 61)

In addition: Discuss your plans for Jesus' birthday party. Will you have a birthday cake? Will you have decorations? Will you have a gift? For whom?

Why Jesus Had to Come

Thursday   FIFTH DAY OF ADVENT

Yesterday we talked about Christmas being Jesus' birthday party. But we did not say very much about *why* Jesus was born.

Do you know why? Why did God's Son Jesus come to earth as a human person, to live like people, like us? We call Jesus our Savior (or saver). From what did we need to be saved?

Way back at the beginning of time, when God made the world and everything in it, He made people to be His special friends. God told them to enjoy the world He had made and live as His friends as He had planned.

But the people weren't satisfied. They wanted to live and do things their own way. That made God angry and sad. He said that because the people had ruined their friendship with Him by not obeying Him, they would die. He sent them away from Him.

Then the people were sorry. They surely needed to be saved. They needed to be saved from death and from their problem of not being God's special friends anymore.

Ever since that time people have all had the same problem. None of us can be God's special friends by ourselves. We all want to do things our own way. We do selfish things that spoil our friendship with God. And we all face the problem of death.

Think about yourself. Tell some ways you make God and people angry. Do you see why you need a Savior? Are you beginning to see why Jesus the Savior was born? We'll talk some more about "why" tomorrow.

Prayer: Come, Lord Jesus, come. We need You to save us from death. We need You to make us God's friends again.

Bible Readings: Genesis 3; Romans 3:10-24

Songs: "Amazing Grace"
"Beautiful Savior"

14

God's Plan and Promise

Friday

Stop for a moment and remember yesterday's reading. We were talking about why Jesus was born, and we did not finish the answer.

Remember how God was angry when the first people sinned by ignoring His rules and doing things their own way? He sent the people away and warned them that they had brought death to the world. But even while God was angry He still loved His people. He didn't zap the people dead on the spot; He let them live a long time and have families and enjoy the world. And before He sent them away from the garden, He helped them put together some clothes.

But even more important, God had a plan for saving the whole world and all people from the curse of death. He didn't tell people the whole plan right away, or make it happen yet. He took His time. While He was waiting, God gave His people hints about His plan. Sometimes He gave them big bright promises—like the one He gave His friend Abraham.

God told Abraham that he and his son and grandsons would be the beginning of a big nation of people. From that nation of people, God said, there would come a most special blessing for the whole world. And what nation of people was Jesus born in? Abraham's nation, called Israel.

Through some other special people called prophets God told more of His plan and made more promises—like when Isaiah announced:

"'But you, Israel, My servant, Jacob, whom I have chosen, the offspring of Abraham, My friend . . . fear not, for I am with you . . . I am your God . . . I will help you,' says the Lord; 'Your Redeemer is the Holy One of Israel'" (Isaiah 41:8, 10, 14).

God's plan was for Jesus to be born as the Holy One of Israel, because of His great love for His people. Just how Jesus became our Redeemer (or Savior) we'll talk about tomorrow.

Prayer: Thank You, God, for loving us. Thank You for planning to save us from the curse of death. Help us always believe Your promises. Come, Lord Jesus Redeemer, come. Amen.

Songs: "God Promised," v. 1 (See page 61)
                          "Of the Father's Love Begotten"

Bible Readings: Genesis 12:1-9; 17:1-8; Jeremiah 31:31-34

In addition: Read the Arch Book, *The Great Promise* (CPH)

How God Kept His Promise

Saturday   SEVENTH DAY OF ADVENT

Hundreds and hundreds of years after Abraham died, when God decided the time was just right, He carried out His special plan. He sent His own Son Jesus to earth to be our Redeemer, just as He had promised.

Read the story of Jesus' birth—the Christmas story—in Luke 1:26-35 and Luke 2:1-11.

Finally—after all those many years of waiting—there He was—the Savior of the world—a teeny tiny baby without a bed. What a surprise! And what good news! Can you think of any better good news in the whole world?

But wait a minute. God's plan wasn't finished yet. Jesus didn't save us from the curse of our sin just by being born. That was only the beginning.

Jesus grew up and lived a full life, the way God His Father wanted life to be lived. Jesus cared for people, healed them, and taught them about God's love and His plan to forgive them. Then He died—but not because *He* had broken God's friendship or done anything wrong. Jesus died because *we* had. He died on purpose to take our death curse for us, and to conquer it. God gave Jesus the power to win over death by coming alive again.

Now the curse of death is broken. We'll still die some day, but we won't stay dead. If we believe Jesus died for us to take our punishment because of God's love for us, we'll come alive again, too. We will live as God's friends forever. That's God's plan and promise for us.

And that's what makes Christmas such a happy celebration. It's the beginning of Easter!

Prayer: Thank You, God, for sending Jesus to break the curse of death for us. For His sake, forgive all our sins. Keep us safe in Your love that we may be Your friends forever. Amen.

Songs: "God Promised" (vv. 1-4) (See page 61)
"Of the Father's Love Begotten"
"I Know That My Redeemer Lives"

Bible Readings: Romans 5:6—6:4; John 3:16

In addition: Personalize John 3:16 by filling the blanks with your own name as you read it aloud. Repeat for each member of the family.
"For God so loved _____ that He gave His only Son, that if _____ believes in Him, _____ will not perish but have eternal life."

Advent 8~17

What Are We Waiting for? Part I— The Coming of Jesus Long Ago

A Crown

Sunday   EIGHTH DAY OF ADVENT

While the people of Israel waited—and waited—and waited— for God to keep His promise and send a Savior, they wondered what this Messiah would be like. They had a long time to think about it, and they came up with many ideas. Some of their ideas came from clues God gave them in the messages of His prophets. Some other ideas came from their own history—from what they knew about God's love in the past. Still other ideas came from their own imaginations—their own ideas about the kind of Messiah, or Savior, they would like God to send them.

One of the most popular ideas about the promised Messiah was that He would be a great king. The people of Israel kept hoping they would be a great nation, in control of their own country. They wanted to be respected and admired by other nations and led by a good and powerful king. That was the kind of Messiah God's people really wanted.

For a while the people of Israel did have good kings to rule them. One of those kings was David. But even David knew he was not the special king God had promised. David sang, "Lift up your heads, O gates! and be lifted up, O ancient doors! that the King of glory may come in. Who is this King of glory? The Lord of hosts, He is the King of glory!" (Psalm 24:9-10).

And the prophet Jeremiah wrote, "Behold, the days are coming, says the Lord, when I will raise up for David a righteous Branch, and He shall reign as king and deal wisely, and shall execute justice and righteousness in the land. In His days Judah will be saved, and Israel will dwell securely. And this is the name by which He will be called. 'The Lord is our Righteousness'" (Jeremiah 23:5-6).

Can you think of a good symbol, or picture, to remind us of these kingly ideas about the promised Messiah? How about a crown? Every time you eat a crown-shaped cookie or see a crown-shaped Christmas ornament it can help you think about Jesus who was born to be our king.

Prayer: Come, Lord Jesus, come. Come and rule our hearts. Come and crown our lives with Your love. Amen.

Bible Readings: Isaiah 28:1-6; Zechariah 9:9-16.

Songs: "King of Glory" (See page 61)
"Lift Up Your Heads, Ye Mighty Gates"

In addition: Serve each member of the family a crown-shaped cookie (Appendix C) and review its symbolism.
Make paper or foil crowns to wear.

Make crown-shaped ornaments to save for your Christmas tree (use whatever materials you prefer—foil, cardboard, styrofoam, glitter, sequins, etc.).

A Rose

Monday   NINTH DAY OF ADVENT

We mentioned yesterday that at times in their history the people of Israel did have their own government, with good kings to rule them. At other times, however, Abraham's nation did not have a land or government of their own. For 40 years the people lived as desert wanderers until God gave them their own country called Canaan.

And many years later, after many wars, the Israelites were forced to live in exile. ("Exile" means that after being captured, they were taken away from their own land. They had to live among strangers who were their enemies.)

Imagine how God's people felt during times like that. Imagine how sad and lonely they were. Imagine how they must have prayed that God would rescue them by sending His promised Messiah.

Some of these feelings and thoughts are told in the song "O Come, O Come, Emmanuel" (see page 62). "Emmanuel" is another name for Jesus, meaning "God is with us." We need Jesus to be with us to rescue us from our sin just as Israel needed to be rescued from exile.

Even in the desert, and even in exile, the people of Israel had God's promises and His prophets to comfort them and give them hope. Some of the promises told of new life, new growth, new blooming for God's people when the Messiah would come.

Through the prophet Hosea God said, "I will heal their faithlessness; I will love them freely, for My anger has turned from them. I will be as the dew to Israel; he shall blossom as the lily . . . . They shall flourish as a garden . . ." (Hosea 14:4-7).

Isaiah wrote, "In days to come Jacob shall take root, Israel shall blossom and put forth shoots, and fill the whole world with fruit" (Isaiah 27:6).

"The desert shall rejoice and blossom; like the crocus it shall blossom abundantly . . . . They shall see the glory of the Lord. . . . He will come and save you" (Isaiah 35:1-4).

For a symbol to remind us of these promises, let's use a flower. It can help us remember God's flower power—His saving love that forgives our sin and lets us bloom with new life and joy.

> O come, O come, Emmanuel,
> And ransom captive Israel that mourns in lonely exile here
> until the Son of God appear.
> Rejoice! Rejoice! Emmanuel shall come to thee, O Israel.

Prayer: Come, Lord Jesus, come. Come and rescue us from the "desert" of our sin. Forgive us. Help us grow and bloom in Your love. Amen.

Songs: "O Come, O Come, Emmanuel," v. 1 (See page 62)
"Behold, a Branch Is Growing"

Bible Readings: Matthew 1:18-23; Isaiah 11; Isaiah 40:3-8

In addition: Serve each member of the family a flower-shaped cookie (Appendix C) and review its symbolism.

Make flower-shaped ornaments to save for your Christmas tree.

Discuss the possibility of having a special floral centerpiece or blooming plant in your home for Christmas.

A Scepter

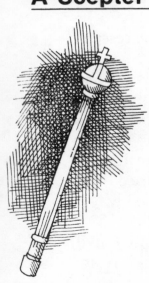

Tuesday   **TENTH DAY OF ADVENT**

Do you remember the ideas about a king that we talked about two days ago? We used a crown as a symbol to remind us of those ideas.

Another symbol for a king is a scepter, a very special rod often made of precious stuff like gold and jewels. A scepter stands for power and authority. The person who holds the scepter is the one who has power to rule the people of that country.

The people of Israel often dreamed of such power, of someone who would rule over them to make them great—especially when they were wandering in the desert or living in lonely exile. They longed for some powerful leader to come and give them victory over their enemies. They needed someone with power to give them victory over death. So do we.

Again, the people of Israel had—and we have—God's promises for such a Savior, someone to rule over our lives with the scepter of God's power and love:

"The scepter shall not depart from Judah, nor the ruler's staff from between his feet, until He comes to whom it belongs, and to Him shall be the obedience of the peoples" (Genesis 49:10).

"I see Him, but not now; I behold Him, but not nigh. . . . A scepter shall rise out of Israel" (Numbers 24:17).

In telling about the Promised One who would come as a scepter-holder, Isaiah said: "To us a Child is born, to us a Son is given; and the government will be upon His shoulder, and His name will be called 'Wonderful Counselor, Mighty God, Everlasting Father, Prince of Peace.' Of the increase of His government and of peace there will be no end, upon the throne of David, and over his kingdom, to establish it and uphold it with justice and with righteousness from this time forth and for evermore" (Isaiah 9:6-7).

Those are powerful names for a child, aren't they? One of God's big surprises was the sending of a tiny baby named Jesus to be the Messiah, the scepter-holder. He turned out to be a king indeed, but a different kind of king from what God's people expected.

As we get closer to Christmas, we'll talk some more about the kind of ruler Jesus is.

> O come, Thou Rod of Jesse,
>   free
> Thine own from Satan's tyranny;
> from depths of hell Thy people save
> and give them victory o'er the grave.
> Rejoice! Rejoice! Emmanuel shall come to thee, O Israel.

Prayer: Come, Lord Jesus, come. Rule our hearts and lives with Your love. Give us victory over death. Amen.

> Hail, hosanna, David's Son!
> Help, Lord, hear our supplication!
> Let Thy kingdom, scepter, crown,
> Bring us blessing and salvation,
> That forever we may sing:
> Hail, hosanna! to our King.
>   ("Come, Thou Precious Ransom, Come," v. 4)

Songs: "O Come, O Come, Emmanuel," v. 2 (See page 62)
"Lift Up Your Heads, Ye Mighty Gates," vv. 1, 2, 3

In addition: Serve each member of the family a scepter-shaped cookie (Appendix C) and review its symbolism.

Make scepter-shaped ornaments to save for your Christmas tree.

A Rising Sun

Wednesday   ELEVENTH DAY OF ADVENT

What does darkness mean to you? How does darkness make you feel? How does it make you feel if you're alone in the dark in a strange place and you don't know what's happening around you? Would you want to be driving at night along a country road with no streetlights and have your car's headlights go out? What would you do?

The Bible often uses darkness and night as symbol language to help explain how it feels to be lost from God because of our sin. And what do you need most when you're lost in the dark? Light, of course.

As the people of Israel waited and waited for the promised Messiah to come, they sometimes thought of Him as a great light. He would be like the sunrise, God said, like a dayspring, the beginning of the day:

"For you who fear My name the sun of righteousness shall rise" (Malachi 4:2).

The prophet Isaiah wrote, "Arise, shine, for your light has come, and the glory of the Lord has risen upon you. For behold, darkness shall cover the earth, and thick darkness the peoples; but the Lord will arise upon you, and His glory will be seen upon you. And nations shall come to your light, and kings to the brightness of your rising" (Isaiah 60:1-3).

Jesus was born to be God's saving light, to guide us through the darkness of death, by dying and rising for the forgiveness of our sin. He himself once said, "I am the Light of the world; he who follows Me will not walk in darkness, but will have the light of life" (John 8:12).

That's why a sunburst or sunrise is another good symbol for the Messiah. It reminds us of more of God's promises and gives meaning to this prayer and hymn verse:

> O come, Thou Day-spring from on high,
> and cheer us by Thy drawing nigh;
> disperse the gloomy clouds of night
> and death's dark shadows put to flight.
> Rejoice! Rejoice! Emmanuel shall come to thee, O Israel.

Prayer: Come, Lord Jesus, come. Brighten our lives with Your love. Lead us through the darkness of death to a new day of life with You. Amen.

Songs: "O Come, O Come, Emmanuel" v. 3 (See page 62)
"Beautiful Savior"

Bible Readings: John 1:1-13; Luke 1:68-79; Luke 2:22-32; Isaiah 60:19-22

In addition: Serve each member of the family a sunrise-shaped cookie (Appendix C), and review its symbolism.

Review the meaning of the candles on your Advent log or wreath. Comment on the symbolism of the increasing brightness of the candlelight as we approach Christmas.

Make sunrise-shaped ornaments to save for your Christmas tree (thin styrofoam cut to shape and covered completely with gold glitter would be simple and effective; for a more elaborate project add rays of tinsel or metallic fringe).

A Key

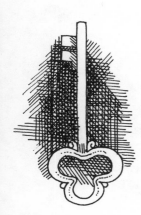

Thursday   TWELFTH DAY OF ADVENT

Have you ever come home and discovered the door was locked . . . and you didn't have a house key . . . and when you knocked and rang the bell, no one came to let you in? Have you ever been locked out of your car with the key locked inside . . . and you had to call someone with a spare key to come and rescue you?

A key is a most important tool, isn't it? When you have the right key, no one else can lock you in where you don't want to be or lock you out of where you have a right to be.

A key, then, is another good symbol to help explain the meaning of the promised Messiah.

When the first people broke God's friendship by choosing to decide for themselves between right and wrong, God locked them out of His garden and sent them away. Ever since then we and all people would have been locked out of God's kingdom because of our own sin—except that . . .

God's plan was to unlock His kingdom again and bring us home to Him. The key to open heaven for us was and is the Promised One, Jesus. By dying in our place and rising again, He made sure the door to God's kingdom will always be open for us. The Father waits with open arms to welcome us home.

Whenever we use a key, or eat a key-shaped Advent cookie, we can remember God's message to John in Revelation 3:7-8, "The words of the holy one, the true one, who has the key of David, who opens and no one shall shut, who shuts and no one opens. I know your works. Behold, I have set before you an open door, which no one is able to shut."

> O come, Thou Key of David,
> come
> and open wide our heavenly home;
> make safe the way that leads on high
> and close the path to misery.
> Rejoice! Rejoice! Emmanuel shall come to thee, O Israel.

Prayer: Come, Lord Jesus, come. Unlock our ears to hear Your Word. Unlock our hearts to believe and trust Your promises. Open wide our heavenly home and lead us safely there. Amen.

> Let all together praise our God
> Before His glorious throne;
> Today He opens heaven again
> To give us His own Son.

> He is the Key, and He the Door
> To blessed Paradise
> The angel bars the way no more.
> To God our praises rise.

Song: "O Come, O Come, Emmanuel," v. 4 (See page 62)

Bible Readings: John 14:1-6; Revelation 4: Hebrews 12:19-23

In addition: Serve each member of the family a key-shaped Advent cookie (Appendix C), and review its symbolism.

Make key-shaped ornaments to save for your Christmas tree.

A Star

What's your favorite star song or poem? Is it "Twinkle, Twinkle, Little Star"? or "Star Light, Star Bright . . ."? or "Catch a Falling Star"? or what? . . . and why?

What is it that makes stars so interesting that we enjoy staring at them for hours? Why do some people write romantic songs about stars? Why do some people think that stars have power to control human lives?

Maybe the reason stars get so much attention is that they are far, far away and mysterious. We really don't understand what stars are and what they mean (as "Twinkle, Twinkle, Little Star" suggests).

In one of the hints God gave His people about the promised Messiah He mentioned a star. The prophet Balaam said, "I see Him, but not now; I behold Him, but not nigh; a star shall come forth out of Jacob, and a scepter shall rise out of Israel" (Numbers 24:17).

As the people of Israel waited and waited for God to keep His promises, the Messiah probably did seem like a star. He was a bright spot in their hopes, but He seemed far, far away and mysterious.

Then Jesus came to earth. "I am the root and offspring of David, the bright morning star," He told John in His Revelation (22:16). No longer was He far, far away and mysterious. He came right up close to His people and lived among them. He preached to them, taught them, and showed them signs so we could know who He was, what He did, and why He lived.

No longer need we say of the Star of Jacob, "How I wonder what you are." We know. He is God's only-begotten Son, given by the Father so that whoever believes in Him may have eternal life (John 3:16).

See how God, for us providing,   Jacob's Star in all its splendor
Gave His Son and life abiding;   Beams with comfort sweet and tender,
He our weary steps is guiding   Forcing Satan to surrender,
From earth's woe to heavenly joy.   Breaking all the powers of hell.

("Come, Your Hearts and Voices Raising," vv. 3, 5)

Prayer:	Come, Lord Jesus, come. Come near to us so we can see clearly who You are. Give us the faith to believe in You as our Lord and Savior. Amen.
Bible Readings:	2 Peter 1:16-19; Psalm 57.
Songs:	"God Promised" vv. 1, 2 (See page 61) "How Lovely Shines the Morning Star"
In addition:	Serve each member of the family a star-shaped Advent cookie (Appendix C) and review its symbolism. Make star-shaped ornaments to save for your Christmas tree.

A Lamb

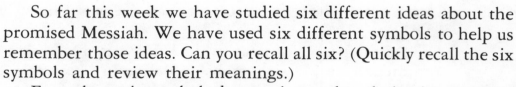

Saturday   FOURTEENTH DAY OF ADVENT

So far this week we have studied six different ideas about the promised Messiah. We have used six different symbols to help us remember those ideas. Can you recall all six? (Quickly recall the six symbols and review their meanings.)

Even those six symbols do not give us the whole picture of the Promised One. There's one more very important idea, one more very important clue God gave His people while they waited and waited for the Messiah to come. That clue came from the prophet Isaiah.

Isaiah described a special servant of the Lord who would suffer and die for the sin of the people. "Like a lamb that is led to slaughter," Isaiah said. "It was the will of the Lord to bruise Him; He has put Him to grief; when He makes Himself an offering for sin, He shall . . . make many to be accounted righteous" (Isaiah 53:7, 10-11).

The sacrifice of a lamb was not a new idea for the people of Israel. God had required them to make sacrifices (give up something precious) as part of their worship—to show their sorrow over their sins, to pray for God's mercy, or to celebrate special thanksgiving and occasions for praise.

But the sacrifice of God's own Lamb—His Son Jesus—to take

away the guilt of our sin—that *was* a new idea. Jesus was born to be that Lamb. When John the Baptizer recognized Jesus, John said, "Behold, the Lamb of God, who takes away the sin of the world" (John 1:29).

Jesus offered Himself into death as the sacrifice for our sin. And then He rose again in victory over death. He made sure for us the promise of eternal life. Now we can all share the apostle John's vision of the Lamb of God sitting in bright glory on His throne in heaven, receiving the praises of all the redeemed—like us.

He died for me. He died for you.	He rose again for me and you.
He died to be our Savior.	He rose to be our Savior.
When Jesus died upon the cross	When Jesus came to life again
God kept His promise true.	God kept His promise true.

Prayer: Come, Lamb of God, come. Come and teach us the meaning of Your sacrifice. Help us believe that it was for us You died. Help us trust Your promise of new life. Amen.

Songs: "God Promised" (See page 61)
"Crown Him with Many Crowns"
"A Lamb Goes Uncomplaining Forth"

Bible Readings: Isaiah 52:13—53:12; Exodus 12:21-32; Revelation 5:6-14

In addition: Serve each member of the family a lamb-shaped Advent cookie (Appendix C) and review its symbolism.

Make lamb-shaped ornaments to save for your Christmas tree.

People Who Waited: Noah

Sunday   FIFTEENTH DAY OF ADVENT

How do rainy days make you feel? How would you feel if it rained for more than a month—like 40 days and nights—and because of the rain you were not allowed to go out? Would you believe the sun was still shining warm and glorious above the rain clouds?

During the many years the people of Israel waited for God to keep His promise of a Messiah, there were other promises they had to wait for besides that big one. It almost seems as if God was training them to wait for Him to keep His Word.

One example of such promise-giving, promise-waiting, and promise-keeping is the story of Noah. Stop and review the story in Genesis 6:11-22; 7:17-24; and 8:6-19.

Noah and his family did a lot of waiting, didn't they? They were able to wait because they trusted God. They trusted His promise that He would save them. They believed God knew what He was doing. They were sure God loved them. They counted on Him to keep His Word.

And He did. God is faithful to His people. He keeps His promises to those who wait for Him. As Noah discovered, God is certainly worth waiting for.

God moves in a mysterious way
His wonders to perform;
He plants His footsteps in the sea
And rides upon the storm.

You fearful saints, fresh courage take;
The clouds you so much dread
Are big with mercy and shall break
In blessings on your head.

(vv. 1, 3)

Prayer: God, thank You for being faithful to Noah. Thank You for being faithful to us. Help us always to trust Your promises. Give us the patience to wait for Your blessings. In Jesus' name. Amen.

Bible Readings: Psalm 93: Psalm 98

Songs: "I Am Trusting Thee, Lord Jesus"
"Noah" songs your children may know from church school experiences

In addition: Read the Arch Book, *Noah's Ark.*

People Who Waited:
Moses and the People of Israel

Monday   SIXTEENTH DAY OF ADVENT

Another example of Old Testament promise-giving, promise-waiting, and promise-keeping is the story of Moses and the people of Israel. Israel's story is much longer than Noah's story. Noah and his family had to wait through 40 days of rain. Moses and the Israelites had to wait through 40 years of desert camping before God kept a special promise to them.

Maybe you remember the story of how Moses helped the Israelites escape from Egypt where they had been slaves for 400 years. God worked a series of miracles to convince the ruler of Egypt to let God's people go free. Finally they made it safely out of Egypt by crossing the Red Sea, while God held the water back and made a path for them (Exodus 13:17—14:31).

God's plan was to give the people a new country to live in—one they could call their own. But once the people were on their way to this new land, they began to doubt God and His promises. Because they broke their promises to trust God, God delayed His promise. He made them wait 40 years before He led them into their Promised Land.

But even during those 40 years God loved His people and cared for them. When the people couldn't find water to drink, God gave Moses the power to work miracles and produce water (Exodus 15:22-25; 17:1-7). When the people complained about hunger and lack of food in the desert, God sent miracle food to satisfy their needs (Exodus 16:2-3, 12-15, 31, 35). The Israelites were not very good at waiting; but God was.

And when the 40 years were done, God led the people safely into their new country—just as He had promised. They learned they could count on God to keep His Word. They discovered God was worth waiting for!

Prayer: God, thank You for being faithful to Moses and the Israelites. Thank You for being faithful to us. Help us always to trust Your promises. Give us the patience to wait for Your blessings. In Jesus' name. Amen.

Bible Readings: Exodus 15:1-13; Psalm 103.

Songs: "I Will Sing of the Mercies of the Lord"
"Our God, Our Help in Ages Past"

In addition: Read the Arch Book, *The Great Escape.*

People Who Waited: Mary and Joseph

Tuesday   SEVENTEENTH DAY OF ADVENT

Finally it happened! After all those years of waiting—hundreds and thousands of years of waiting—God decided it was the right time to keep His most special promise. He sent an angel to earth to announce that the Messiah, the Promised Savior, would be born.

The angel came to a young woman named Mary. She was the one God had chosen to be the mother of Jesus. Read what the angel said in Luke 1:26-35.

What great news that was! Imagine how Mary must have felt! But did you notice something? The angel did not hand Mary a precious bundle and say, "Here is Jesus, your instant baby." No, even Mary had to wait—not as little as 40 days like Noah, or as much as 40 years like Moses, but 40 weeks like your own mother when she waited for you to be born.

Mary had to wait to give birth to Jesus, but she just couldn't wait to share the good news. She rushed off to visit her cousin Elizabeth and tell her about God's most special promise. Read Mary's happy song in Luke 1:46-55. Notice especially the last line.

Mary believed that what was happening to her was God's way of remembering the promise He had made to the people of Israel, to Abraham, and all the rest. She was able to wait because she trusted God. She knew she could count on Him to keep His Word. She was sure of His great love and mercy. Are you?

God, thank You for being faithful to Mary. Thank You for being faithful to us. Help us always to trust Your promises. Give us the patience to wait for Your blessings. And help us to celebrate while we wait. In Jesus' Name. Amen.

Bible Readings: Isaiah 7:13-14; 1 Chronicles 16:8-34

Songs: "God Promised," vv 1-4 (See page 61)

In addition: Read the Arch Book, *Mary's Story.*

Now thank we all our God
With heart and hands and voices,
Who wondrous things hath done,
In whom His world rejoices;
Who from our mother's arms
Hath blessed us on our way
With countless gifts of love
And still is ours today.

Oh, may this bounteous God
Thro' all our life be near us,
With ever joyful hearts
And blessed peace to cheer us
And keep us in His grace
And guide us when perplexed
And free us from all ills
In this world and the next!

All praise and thanks to God
The Father now be given,
The Son, and Him who reigns
With them in highest heaven:
The one eternal God,
Whom earth and heav'n adore!
For thus it was, is now,
And shall be evermore.

Advent 18~21

What Are We Waiting for? Part II—The Coming of Jesus Today

Jesus Comes to Us by His Spirit

Wednesday   EIGHTEENTH DAY OF ADVENT

When Mary's 40 weeks of waiting were finished, Jesus was born—just as God had promised. Jesus lived His life on earth, died for our sin, rose again in victory, and returned to His Father in heaven. That all happened hundreds of years ago.

So Jesus has already come and gone. And yet, during all these days of Advent, we have been praying "Come, Lord Jesus, come." Do you know why that is? Has that prayer confused you?

We know Jesus won't be born again as a baby on Christmas. We know Christmas is the celebration of His long-ago birthday. But there are other ways Jesus will come to us again on Christmas, just as He comes to us today and everyday.

One of the ways Jesus comes to us now is by His Spirit. And that's another story of promise-giving, promise-waiting, and promise-keeping. Before Jesus died He promised His disciples that He would send His Spirit to comfort them (that is, make them like a strong "fort"), to help them remember and understand His teachings, to keep them in faith, and to give them power and courage for sharing the Good News of the forgiveness of sins.

After Jesus rose from death and went back to heaven, the

disciples waited and worried. They worried and waited. And then, sure enough, Jesus did send His Spirit to the disciples, just as He had promised.

That same Holy Spirit is with us now. It is Jesus' Holy Spirit who works faith in us. It is Jesus' Holy Spirit who teaches us the meaning of God's love and forgiveness. It is Jesus' Holy Spirit who gives us power to forgive others and share the Good News of God's love. It is the Holy Spirit who keeps Jesus' promise "I am with you always, even to the end of the world."

Prayer: Come, Lord Jesus, come. Come by Your Spirit to live in us. Fill our lives with Your love. Give us the power to share Your Good News. Amen.

> Redeemer, come! I open wide
> My heart to Thee; here Lord abide.
> Let me Thine inner presence feel,
> Thy grace and love in me reveal.
>
> Thy Holy Spirit guide us on
> Until our glorious goal is won.
> Eternal praise and fame
> We offer to Thy Name.

Songs: "God Promised," v. 5 (See page 61)
"O Holy Spirit, Enter In"
"Holy Spirit, Hear Us"

Bible Readings: John 14:15-17, 25-27; Acts 2:1-39.

In addition: Review symbols for the Holy Spirit—wind and fire (Acts 2:1-4), dove (John 1:29-34). Discuss how these symbols will be evident at Christmas time (wintry winds, candles, fireplace, tree ornaments, Christmas cards, etc.). Discuss how these symbols can help remind you that Jesus comes to us today by His Spirit.

Jesus Comes to Us in His Word

Thursday   NINETEENTH DAY OF ADVENT

Yesterday we read how Jesus comes to us by His Holy Spirit living in us. Here's a hint today how Jesus comes to us another way:

(Jesus said), "Heaven and earth will pass away, but My words will not pass away" (Mark 13:31).

Sometime later the apostle Paul preached, "God has brought to Israel a Savior, Jesus, as He promised . . . . God raised Him from the dead; and for many days He appeared to those who came up with Him from Galilee to Jerusalem, who are now His witnesses to the people. And we bring you the Good News that what God promised to the fathers, this He has fulfilled to us their children by raising Jesus . . . .

"As they went out, the people begged that these things might be told them the next sabbath . . . . The next sabbath almost the whole city gathered together to hear the Word of God. . . . And the Word of the Lord spread throughout all the region" (Acts 13:23-49).

Did you get the message? Jesus comes to us today, on Christmas, and forever through His Word. Whenever we read and study the Bible, hear God's Word taught, speak it to one another, and share the Good News of our salvation—like right now—Jesus is right here with us.

Before He died, Jesus told His disciples, "If a man loves Me, he will keep My word, and My Father will love him, and We will come to him and make Our home with him" (John 14:23). That's a wonderful promise, isn't it?

And we know God keeps His promises. We know God keeps His Word!

Prayer: Come, Lord Jesus, come. Come to us through Your Word and make Your home with us. Help us to treasure Your Word and share the Good News of our salvation. Amen.

> Ah, dearest Jesus, holy Child,
> Make Thee a bed, soft, undefiled,
> Within my heart, that it may be
> A quiet chamber kept for Thee.

Bible Readings: John 15:3-11; Psalm 130; Revelation 22:6-9.

Songs: "Thy Strong Word Did Cleave the Darkness"
"Jesus Loves Me, This I Know"

Jesus Comes to Us in Sacraments

Friday

Here we are again—yet—still—waiting—always waiting—waiting for Christmas, waiting to celebrate Jesus' coming long ago, waiting for Jesus to come today.

We've talked about how Jesus comes to us today by His Spirit and through His Word. But there's more. There's another and very special way Jesus comes—a way that connects Jesus, some of His words, and the presence of His Holy Spirit with some things, some actions, and with people. This special way of Jesus' coming is called a sacrament.

In the Sacrament of Baptism the *thing* we see is water, and the *action* we see is someone getting wet. The *words of Jesus* connected with the water and the action are: "He who believes and is baptized will be saved" (Mark 16:16), and "Go therefore and make disciples of all nations, baptizing them in the name of the Father and of the Son and of the Holy Spirit" (Matthew 28:19). The action we don't see is Jesus coming to live in the person, the Holy Spirit putting new life into the person, bringing him or her the gift of faith, and claiming that person as a new member of God's family.

In the Sacrament of the Lord's Supper, the *things* are bread and wine, and the *action* is eating and drinking. The *words of Jesus* connected with this sacrament are: "Take, eat; this is My body. . . . Drink of it, all of you; for this is My blood of the covenant, which is poured out for many for the forgiveness of sins" (Matthew 26:26-28). The action we don't see is Jesus coming with His true body and blood into people, and the Holy Spirit coming into the souls of the persons who share in the Lord's Supper, reminding them of Jesus' death and resurrection and bringing them the gift of the forgiveness of sins.

Do you wonder how we know that the action we don't see is really happening? How do we know that, by His Spirit, Jesus is really coming to us in the sacraments?

Well, we simply have to take His Word for it! We simply go on trusting that God always will be as He always has been, the God who keeps His promises and blesses His people with His love. And He *has* promised, "I am with you always, to the close of the age" (Matthew 28:20).

Prayer: Come, Lord Jesus, come. Come to us through Your sacraments. Give us the faith to believe Your words of promise and trust in Your forgiveness. Thank You for claiming us and keeping us in Your family. Amen.

> For the joy Your advent gives us,
> For Your Holy Precious Word,
> For Your Baptism which now saves us,
> For Your Holy Supper, Lord,
> For Your death, the bitter scorn,
> For Your resurrection morn,
> Lord, we thank You and adore You
> And in heaven we shall behold You.

Bible Readings: Galatians 3:26-29; Romans 6:3-5; 1 Corinthians 11:23-26.

Songs: "Baptized into Thy Name Most Holy"
"O Lord, We Praise Thee"
"Let All Mortal Flesh Keep Silence"
"Now"

In addition: Talk about the history and celebrations of baptisms in your family. Has everyone been baptized? When? Do you celebrate your "baptism birthdays"? If so, how and why? If not, how might you do it in the future? (E.g., special baptism candle to light, crown to wear, scallop-shell-shaped cookies to eat, small gift to present, special family devotions, etc.)

Jesus Comes to Us in People

Saturday   **TWENTY-FIRST DAY IN ADVENT**

There's one more way Jesus comes today, on Christmas, and every day—one more way we haven't exactly explained yet. But by now it should be obvious. Do you know what it is?

You're it! And so am I. Jesus comes to us through people. After all, it's people in whom His Holy Spirit lives. It's people who read and study and teach and share His holy Word. It's people who are baptized and share in the eating and drinking of His Holy Supper. It's people through whom Jesus comes to us today.

These are some ways the Bible describes the idea of Jesus coming in people:

"Now you are the body of Christ and individually members of it" (1 Corinthians 12:27).

"Do you not know that you are God's temple and that God's Spirit dwells in you?" (1 Corinthians 3:16).

"I am the vine, and you the branches. He who dwells in Me, as I dwell in him, bears much fruit; for apart from Me you can do nothing" (John 15:5 NEB).

"The King will answer, 'I tell you this; anything you did for one of My brothers here, however humble, you did for Me'" (Matthew 25:40 NEB).

"Where two or three are gathered together in My name, there am I in the midst of them" (Matthew 18:20 KJV).

And that's pretty close!

That's one reason we send each other Christmas cards and give each other Christmas gifts. When we send someone a Christmas card, it's like sending a birthday card to Jesus-living-in-them. When you give me a Christmas present, it's like giving a birthday present to Jesus-living-in-me. And I give birthday presents to Jesus-living-in-you.

One last thought—do you ever have to wait for someone in your family? one of your friends? someone at school or at work? If you remember that Jesus is coming to you through people, would it make waiting easier? Would that person be worth waiting for?

Prayer: Come, Lord Jesus, come. Come to us in people; teach us to recognize You in people. Help us love each other as we would love You. Help us receive each other's love as a gift from You. Amen.

> O Holy Child of Bethlehem,
> Descend to us, we pray;
> Cast out our sin and enter in,
> Be born in us today.

Bible Reading: Matt. 25:31-46.

Songs: "God Promised," especially v. 5 (See page 61)
"Whatsoever You Do"

In addition: If you have not already begun making "people-ornaments" for your Christmas tree, you might now choose to do so. See Appendix B and "Second Day of Advent."

Advent 22~28

What Are We Waiting for? Part III— The Coming of Jesus Again Someday

Jesus Promises to Return

Sunday   TWENTY-SECOND DAY OF ADVENT

Hurray! This is the week! After all this waiting, Christmas is almost here. Soon we'll be lighting the tree, giving and opening gifts, singing those favorite carols, and enjoying special treats. Our waiting is almost over.

Or is it? When Christmas is said and done, will there be anything else to wait for?

The answer, of course, is YES. We have another promise from God—a super special promise—for which we wait. It's a promise Jesus made before He died, rose again in victory over death, and returned to live in glory with His Father in heaven.

Jesus promised, "I go to prepare a place for you. . . . I will come again and will take you to Myself, that where I am you may be also" (John 14:2-3).

That's quite a promise. It's a promise of eternal life. It's a promise of glory and joy far beyond anything we can imagine. The apostle John wrote a *whole book* just trying to describe a vision he had seen of what the return of Jesus would be like.

Jesus Himself also talked about returning to earth with power and great glory. And then He explained, "The King will say . . . ,

'Come, O blessed of My Father, inherit the kingdom prepared for you from the foundation of the world'" (Matthew 25:34).

Imagine that! We think we've been waiting a long time—God's been waiting for us since the beginning of the world! And one of these days He'll come back—the King of kings, the Lord of lords, the Ruler of heaven and earth, in great beauty, splendor, and power—and simply say, "Come home."

Now that's worth waiting for, isn't it?

Prayer: Come, Lord Jesus, come. Amen!

Songs: "King of Glory" (See page 61)
                "O Come, O Come, Emmanuel" (See page 62)

Bible Readings: Matthew 25:31-46; John 14.

"We're Expecting" Again/Yet

Monday   TWENTY-THIRD DAY OF ADVENT

So here we are, expecting again. Even after Christmas we'll still be waiting—waiting for Jesus to come again. What's it like to live in constant expectation? What do we do while we wait?

While we wait, we celebrate! While we wait for Jesus to come again we celebrate that He came and comes. While we wait for God to keep more promises, we celebrate that He did and does keep other promises. While we wait for the future to happen, we celebrate what happened long ago and is happening every day. We even celebrate the future NOW. That's how sure we are of God's promises.

That's what our Christmas celebration is all about. We retell the old, old story of Jesus' birth. We sing the song of the angels. We go with the shepherds to Bethlehem and see the Baby in the manger. With the Wise Men we follow the star and bring gifts to worship the new King. And as we retell this old, old story—maybe even act it out—we remember that the last chapter has not yet been written. We're still waiting for Jesus to come again. We're still waiting for the surprise ending. God seems to like to surprise us. We can be sure that it will be a good surprise.

What do you think will happen? What do you expect?

Prayer: Make me to know Your ways, O Lord; teach me Your paths. Lead me in Your truth, and teach me, for You are the God of my salvation; for You I wait all day long (Psalm 25:4-5).

> Jesus, Thy Church with longing eyes
> For Thine expected coming waits.
> When will the promised light arise
> And glory beam from Zion's gates?
>
> Teach us in watchfulness and prayer
> To wait for the appointed hour
> And fit us by Thy grace to share
> The triumphs of Thy conquering power.

Songs: "Lift Up Your Heads, Ye Mighty Gates"
Begin practicing Christmas carols and hymns.

Bible Readings: Matthew 24:29-31, 42-44; 1 Thessalonians 4:13-18; Revelation 22:6-21

How the Early Church Waited for Jesus' Return

Tuesday   **TWENTY-FOURTH DAY OF ADVENT**

The disciples and other friends of Jesus believed His promise to come again. They lived from day to day expecting Jesus to return in power and glory. They thought He might come again at any moment.

But they didn't just sit around doing nothing. They didn't stand and stare at the sky. While they waited they celebrated. They celebrated by sharing the Good News of forgiveness with many other people. They told others about Jesus' promises of new life with Him.

And those who believed the Good News were soon too many to count. Thousands were baptized. Now thousands were waiting for Jesus to come again. And while these new Christians waited, they celebrated!

Here's how the Bible reports their celebrations:
"They devoted themselves to the apostles' teaching

(Jesus comes to us in His Word—remember?)
and fellowship (Jesus comes to us in people),
to the breaking of bread
(Jesus comes to us in the sacraments)
and the prayers . . . (Come, Lord Jesus, come!)
*with glad and generous hearts, praising God and having favor
with all the people"* (Acts 2:42-47).
(While we wait we celebrate!)

Prayer: Come, Lord Jesus, come. Come and make our hearts glad and generous. Keep us faithful until You come again in glory and power. Amen.

Bible Readings: Acts 2:37-47; 2 Thessalonians 2.

Songs: "The Advent of Our King"
"The King Shall Come When Morning Dawns"

Apostles' Doctrine: While We Wait

Wednesday   TWENTY-FIFTH DAY OF ADVENT

While the early Christians waited for Jesus to come again they "continued in the apostles' doctrine." They listened and studied. They read and learned more about God's promises and how He kept those promises in Jesus. And the more they knew about Jesus, the more they told others. What they believed, they shared.

You can do the same thing. Try it. Review what you have learned about God's promises. Tell what you believe about Jesus, the Promised One. On a separate piece of paper write down in your own words a simple statement of your faith. Be sure everyone in the family contributes something to the statement. Try to make sure that eveyone agrees with all that you write into your statement of faith. Be sure your ideas agree with God's Word.

Then, on Christmas Day, when you gather for family devotions, read your version of God's Word—your family's "doctrine." By sharing your faith, you will be celebrating the coming of Jesus— while you wait for Him to come again.

Prayer:	Come, Lord Jesus, come. Come as the living Word. Teach us Your Father's love. Give us Your Spirit's power to share Your Good News with others. Amen.
Bible Readings:	John 20:30-31; Matthew 28:16-20.
Songs:	Practice/learn a "new" Christmas carol or hymn.

Prayer: While We Wait

Thursday   TWENTY-SIXTH DAY OF ADVENT

While the early Christians waited for Jesus to come again, they "continued . . . in the prayers." What do you suppose their prayers were about? For *what* do you think they prayed? For *whom* do you think they prayed?

You can do the same thing. On a separate piece of paper write in your own words some simple prayers. Consider all kinds of prayer thoughts—thanks, praise, needs, forgiveness, people, etc. Be sure everyone in the family gets a turn to add ideas.

Save your written prayers for Christmas Day, when you gather for family devotions. By praying together, you'll be celebrating the coming of Jesus—while you wait for Him to come again.

Prayer:	Come, Lord Jesus, come. Come and teach us to pray. Amen.
Bible Readings:	Colossians 4:2-6; John 17.
Songs:	Learn/practice a "new" Christmas carol or hymn.

Fellowship: While We Wait

Friday   TWENTY-SEVENTH DAY OF ADVENT

While the early Christians waited for Jesus to come again they "continued . . . in fellowship." For them fellowship meant many things. It meant sharing what they owned, worshiping together, eating together, caring for one another, making new friends, sharing each other's joy and sadness, and so on. Their fellowship was a sign of God's love alive in them.

Read Paul's description of fellowship in Colossians 3:1-17. Do his ideas about fellowship sound anything like your own?

How do your ideas about fellowship fit in with your plans for celebrating Christmas? Will you be going to church to worship? Having a party? Going to visit someone special? Giving presents? Sharing what you own with needy people? . . . ? . . . ?

Will your Christmas celebration be a sign of God's love alive in you—while you wait for Jesus to come again?

Prayer: Come, Lord Jesus, come. Bring us Your love and peace and joy. Teach us how to celebrate while we wait. Amen.

Bible Reading: Ephesians 3:14-21

Songs: Learn/practice a "new" Christmas carol or hymn.

Breaking of Bread: While We Wait

Saturday   TWENTY-EIGHTH DAY OF ADVENT

While the early Christians waited for Jesus to come again they "continued . . . in the breaking of bread." This means both friendly fellowship meals and the Lord's Supper. These Christians also continued in Baptism. They knew and trusted God's promises. They believed Jesus was coming to them with His special blessings in the sacraments. St. Paul wrote, "The cup of blessing which we bless, is it not a participation in the blood of Christ? The bread which we break, is it not a participation in the body of Christ?" (1 Corinthians 10:16).

Will you be sharing in the sacraments this Christmas? If so, review their meaning and importance for you.

Since "the breaking of bread" can mean any meal—supper—or lunch—or snack—which is shared in love, talk about how you will be "breaking bread" this Christmas. Do you have any special foods that are a tradition in your family? Will you have a "Jesus' birthday" cake? How will the "breaking of bread" help you celebrate Jesus' coming—while you wait?

Prayer: Come, Lord Jesus, come. Come and nourish us with Your blessings. Amen.

Bible Reading: John 6:47-59.

Songs: Learn/practice a "new" Christmas carol or hymn.

Christmas 1~12
The Christmas Story and Carols in Close-up Images

CHRISTMAS DAY

Merry Christmas!
Today* you're on your own:

—Retell your favorite version of the Christmas Gospel (Luke 2:1-20).

—Share your faith using the words of your own creed (Advent 25). (If you have not written one, improvise one or recite one you already know.)

—Offer your own prayers (Advent 26).

—Sing your very most favorite Christmas songs.

And have a joyous celebration of Jesus' birthday—while you wait.

* (Tomorrow we'll begin a series of close-ups—brief meditations on specific, single images in the Christmas picture.)

44

Mary and Joseph

And **Joseph** also went up from Galilee, from the city of Nazareth, to Judea, to the city of David, which is called Bethlehem, because he was of the house and lineage of David, to be enrolled with **Mary** his betrothed, who was with child. (Luke 2:4-5)

Who were these people, really? By what design—or could it have been by accident—did they become the parents of Jesus?

Luke makes a point of telling us that Joseph's family connections went all the way back to King David. Look at those family connections in Matthew 1:1-16. Matthew traces Joseph's family all the way back to Abraham!

So what's the point? The point is that Joseph and Mary were people of promise. Do you remember the promise God gave to Abraham? We talked about it during the first week of Advent (sixth day). Joseph and Mary were part of God's plan to bless the world through Abraham's family. Their baby Jesus was Abraham's great-great-great-great-great-great-great-(let's skip a few)-great-great-grandson!

But there were thousands of other people who had the same family connections. God could have kept His promise through some other relatives of Abraham and David. All we know is that He didn't. He chose Mary and Joseph. He picked them out of all the rest. They were no accident.

Do you remember the story of the angel coming to Mary? The angel told her she was God's choice, His favorite person for the job of being Jesus' mother. The angel didn't explain. Mary was simply told, "You're it." And Mary believed the promise that God would be with her and make miracles happen to her by His power.

We've been chosen by God, too—but not because of any special family connections here on earth. We're in God's family now because Jesus came to be our Brother. He claims us all as children of His Father in heaven.

And that's the best family connection there is!

Prayer: God, thank You for sending Jesus to be our Brother. Thank You for chosing us to be in Your family. Keep us close in Your love forever. Amen.

To be read or sung:

1. Of the Father's love begotten
   Ere the worlds began to be,
   He is Alpha and Omega,
   He the Source, the Ending He,
   Of the things that are, that have been,
   And that future years shall see
   Evermore and evermore.

2. Oh, that birth forever blessed
   When the Virgin, full of grace,
   By the Holy Ghost conceiving,
   Bare the Savior of our race,
   And the Babe, the world's Redeemer,
   First revealed His sacred face
   Evermore and evermore.

3. O ye heights of heaven adore Him;
   Angel hosts, His praises sing;
   Powers, dominions, bow before Him
   And extol our God and King.
   Let no tongue on earth be silent,
   Every voice in concert ring
   Evermore and evermore.

Bible Readings: Galatians 4:4-7; Matthew 1:18-25; Luke 8:19-21

In addition: Read the Arch Book, *Mary's Story.*

Bethlehem

THIRD DAY OF CHRISTMAS

. . . from Galilee, from the city of Nazareth, to Judea, to the city of David, which is called **Bethlehem** . . . (Luke 2:4)

Bethlehem—just a little town, down the road a piece from Jerusalem, a bigger and busier and far more important city. What was so special about Bethlehem?

What was special about Bethlehem before then was that David had lived there. And through King David God had shown His love and sent great blessings to the people of Israel.

What's special about Bethlehem since then is that Jesus was born there. And through Jesus God showed His love and sent great blessings to the whole world.

What's special about *any* town is who lives there, and how God shows His love and sends His blessings through the person who lives there.

God's style is to act through human history. That means right here in our neighborhood, right now today, God is acting through us to show His love and send His blessings. Our address may never be famous, like "Bethlehem" or "The White House." But our home is special—because God lives here, in us.

Prayer: God, thank You for sending Jesus into our history. Use us here and now to be Your agents for sharing Your love and blessings. In Jesus' Name. Amen.

To be sung or read:

O little town of Bethlehem,
How still we see thee lie!
Above thy deep and dreamless sleep
The silent stars go by.
Yet in thy dark streets shineth
The everlasting light;
The hopes and fears of all the years
Are met in thee tonight.

O holy Child of Bethlehem,
Descend to us, we pray;
Cast out our sin and enter in,
Be born in us today.
We hear the Christmas angels
The great glad tidings tell;
Oh, come to us, Abide with us,
Our Lord Immanuel!

Bible Readings: Micah 5:2-4; Isaiah 42:5-13

In addition: If you have a map of Palestine (check your Bibles, an encyclopedia, or world atlas), locate Bethlehem and trace Mary and Joseph's travels.

Talk about other places where you have lived. What do you remember about them? How—through whom—did you experience God's love at other times and places?

Manger/Stable

FOURTH DAY OF CHRISTMAS

She gave birth to her first-born Son and wrapped Him in swaddling cloths, and laid Him in a **manger,** because there was no place for them in the inn. (Luke 2:7)

Look closely at the manger. Do you see a nice soft mattress there? Or clean smooth sheets? Or a warm cuddly blanket? Does it look like a comfortable bed? Is it in a clean safe hospital nursery? Or even in an ordinary cozy house?

Of course not. Jesus didn't come to earth to be cozy and ordinary, clean and safe, comfortable and cuddly. He came to earth to suffer and die because of our sins. He came to be the "Bread of Life," to feed our souls with His Father's love. And His first bed was a sign, a symbol of what He would be.

Look again at the manger. Do you know what it was usually used for (when there wasn't a strange baby parked in it)? It held hay, food for sheep and cattle. The manger was the animals' feeding trough, their "bread basket."

And there lies the Bread of Life, Baby Jesus! Amazing, isn't it? Amazing grace!

Prayer: God, thank You for sending Jesus to die for us. Help us remember we are not here just to be comfortable, but to be Your servants. Let us be Your love at work even in the strangest places. Amen.

To be sung or read:

Away in a manger,	Be near me, Lord Jesus,
No crib for a bed,	I ask Thee to stay
The little Lord Jesus	Close by me forever
Laid down His sweet head;	And love me, I pray;
The stars in the sky	Bless all the dear children
Looked down where He lay,	In Thy tender care,
The little Lord Jesus	And take us to heaven
Asleep on the hay.	To live with Thee there.

Bible Readings: Luke 9:18-26, 57-62.

In addition: Read the Arch Book, *Benjamin and the First Christmas.*

Baby Jesus

FIFTH DAY OF CHRISTMAS

To you is born this day in the city of David a Savior, who is Christ the Lord. And this will be a sign for you: you will find a **babe** wrapped in swaddling cloths . . . (Luke 2:12)

Jesus was a baby;	I wonder why?
So was I.	I wonder why God made Him be
My Savior was a baby;	A tiny baby just like me?

(Reprinted from *Happy Times,* June '76, CPH)

The Baby announced by the angel was God Himself. As God He had already been alive forever and ever. But now, as Jesus, He was born on earth. He was also a human being.

That's a mystery, isn't it? How could God, who created the whole world and all of life, be a tiny baby?

The reason, though, is no mystery. The angel had told Joseph earlier that the baby would be born to save His people from their sins. To be our Savior, Jesus was born into our human family.

For us to be saved, we need to be born into God's family. When Jesus was a grown-up teacher He said, "Unless one is born of water and the Spirit, he cannot enter the kingdom of God" (John 3:15). That's a mystery, too. But it's a mystery we can trust. God promised that by Baptism and by the power of Jesus' Holy Spirit living in us we have been "born" into His family and made His children.

And we know God keeps His promises. After all, Jesus was born.

Prayer: God, thank You for sending Jesus to be born into our family. Thank You for choosing us to be born by Your Spirit into Your family. Keep us close in Your love forever. Amen.

To be sung or read:

What Child is this who laid to rest
On Mary's lap is sleeping?
Whom angels greet with anthems sweet
While shepherds watch are keeping?
This, this is Christ the King
Whom shepherds guard and angels sing:
Haste, haste to bring Him laud,
The Babe, the Son of Mary.

Why lies He in such mean estate
Where ox and ass are feeding?
Good Christians, fear; for sinners here
The silent Word is pleading.
Nails, spear shall pierce Him through,
The cross be borne for me, for you;
Hail, hail the Word made flesh,
The Babe, the Son of Mary.

Bible Readings: John 1:1-14; 3:1-17.

In addition: Read the Arch Book, *The Baby Born in a Stable.*

Angels

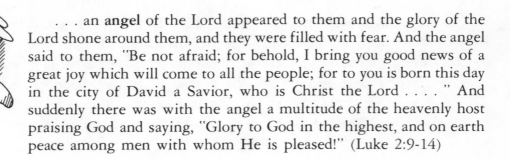

. . . an **angel** of the Lord appeared to them and the glory of the Lord shone around them, and they were filled with fear. And the angel said to them, "Be not afraid; for behold, I bring you good news of a great joy which will come to all the people; for to you is born this day in the city of David a Savior, who is Christ the Lord . . . ." And suddenly there was with the angel a multitude of the heavenly host praising God and saying, "Glory to God in the highest, and on earth peace among men with whom He is pleased!" (Luke 2:9-14)

"Be an angel and . . ." is how some grown-ups start telling children to behave. The sentence usually ends with something like " . . . sit still, keep quiet, and look pretty" or " . . . bring me the newspaper and turn on the television."

Look at the angels in the Christmas story. They were big, bright, and scary. They came in a blast of light that filled the night sky with the glory of the Lord. And they came on a super special mission—to announce the birth of Jesus, our Savior. They were God's special-delivery messengers to bring the good news of peace and shout His praises.

God's given us the same job to do. He's told us to spread His Word and share the Good News of our Savior. We, too, can shout His praises and bring peace to people. We won't light up the night sky or make a big splash on the 5 o'clock news. But we will light up someone's dim view of life. The Gospel we share does change people and bring them peace with God.

So go ahead—"be an angel and . . . " tell someone the Good News about Jesus.

Prayer: God, thank You for sending the angels to announce the birth of our Savior. Thank You for giving us Your Word to share with others. Help us be Your messengers. Amen.

To be sung or read:

Hark! the herald angels sing,
"Glory to the newborn King;
Peace on earth and mercy mild,
God and sinners reconciled!"
Joyful, all ye nations, rise,
Join the triumph of the skies;
With th' angelic hosts proclaim,
"Christ is born in Bethlehem!"
Hark! the herald angels sing,
"Glory to the newborn King!"

Hail, the heavenly Prince of Peace!
Hail, the Sun of Righteousness!
Light and life to all He brings,
Ris'n with healing in His wings.
Mild He leaves His throne on high,
Born that man no more may die;
Born to raise the sons of earth;
Born to give them second birth.
Hark! the herald angels sing,
"Glory to the newborn King!"

Bible Readings: Isaiah 52:7-10; Isaiah 40:1-11; Ephesians 3:7-9.

In addition: Read the Arch Book, *The Night the Angels Sang.*

Shepherds

SEVENTH DAY OF CHRISTMAS

When the angels went away from them into heaven, the **shepherds** said to one another, "Let us go over to Bethlehem and see this thing that has happened, which the Lord has made known to us." And they went with haste, and found Mary and Joseph, and the Babe lying in a manger. And when they saw it, they made known the saying which had been told them concerning this child; . . . And the shepherds returned, glorifying and praising God for all they had heard and seen. (Luke 2:15-20)

Pretend you are those shepherds. Imagine how you would have felt when the angel appeared. Would you have reacted the same way they did?

Would you have believed the angel's news? Would you have left your sheep in the fields and gone into town to find a baby? Would you have dared to tell anyone else that you had seen and heard angels in the sky? Would you have gone back to work singing praises to God?

Pretend you are the townspeople of Bethlehem. Imagine what you would have thought when you heard the shepherds' story.

Would you have believed they saw angels? Would you have

51

believed their story about who the baby in the manger was? Would you have followed them to see for yourself? Would you have joined them in praising God for His marvelous gift of a Savior?

The response of the shepherds is a good example for all of us to follow:

—to hear and believe the Good News that Jesus is born to be our Savior,

—to spread that Good News to everyone around us,

—to praise and worship God for His marvelous Gift even while doing our daily work.

Sounds almost like the work of angels, doesn't it?

Prayer: God, give us the faith to believe Jesus is our Savior. Give us the faith to share Your Good News with others. Give us the faith to worship and praise you in all we do. In Jesus' Name. Amen.

To be sung or read:

O come, all ye faithful, joyful and triumphant,
O come ye, O come ye to Bethlehem;
Come and behold Him, born the king of angels;
O come, let us adore Him, O come, let us adore Him,
O come, let us adore Him, Christ the Lord.

Yea, Lord, we greet Thee, born this happy morning.
Jesus, to Thee be all glory given.
Word of the Father, now in flesh appearing;
O come, let us adore Him, O come, let us adore Him,
O come, let us adore Him, Christ the Lord.

Bible Readings: Romans 1:15-17; Ephesians 1:3-4; Psalm 150.

The Star

EIGHTH DAY OF CHRISTMAS

Now when Jesus was born, . . . Wise Men from the East came to Jerusalem, saying, "Where is He who has been born King of the Jews? For we have seen His **star** in the East, and have come to worship Him" . . . . And lo, the star which they had seen in the East went before them, till it came to rest over the place where the Child was. (Matthew 2:1-9)

One time when Jesus was with His disciples in a boat on a lake, a sudden storm came on them. Big waves splashed into the boat. The men were afraid they would sink. Jesus said to the wind and the waves "Be still!" And they were. And the people wondered aloud, "Who then is this, that even wind and sea obey Him?" (Mark 4:35-41).

When Jesus was born, a bright new star appeared in the sky. Wise Men in the East noticed the star. They recognized it as a sign that something special was happening. Who then is this, that even a star announces His birth?

When Jesus died on the cross for our sins, daylight disappeared. The sky grew dark and an earthquake shook the land. Who then is this, that even the earth and the sky mourn His death?

The soldier standing guard at the cross declared, "Truly this was the Son of God!" The Wise Men recognized His star and asked, "Where is He who has been born King of the Jews?"

There He is in the manger. There He is in the boat. There He is on the cross. There He is, alive again, greeting His friends on Easter. There He is, ascending into heaven. Here He is, living in you and me. Here He is, with the power of His Spirit, making *us* signs of His love alive in the world. Here He is, the Star of Jacob, the Light of the world, shining in us, making us His stars, leading others to worship Him!

Prayer: God, thank You for all the signs and wonders that lead us to You. Give us the faith to recognize Jesus as our Savior. Help us to be signs of Your love and lead others to worship You. Amen.

To be sung or read:

> We three kings of Orient are,
> Bearing gifts, we traverse afar
> Field and fountain, moor and mountain,
> Following yonder star.
> O star of wonder, star of night,
> Star with royal beauty bright,
> Westward leading, still proceeding,
> Guide us to thy perfect Light.

Bible Readings: Isaiah 60:1-3; Revelation 21:22-26

In addition: Read the Arch Book, *The Secret of the Star.*

Wise Men

. . . behold Wise Men from the East came to Jerusalem saying, "Where is He who is born King of the Jews? For we have seen His **star** in the East and have come to worship Him." . . . And lo, the star which they had seen in the East went before them, till it came to rest over the place where the Child was. When they saw the star, they rejoiced with great joy; and going into the house they fell down and worshiped Him. (Matthew 2:1-2, 9-11)

"I will make of you a great nation," God promised Abraham, "and in you all the families of the earth shall be blessed" (Genesis 12:2-3).

Notice that? All families of the earth. God's promise of blessing was not only for the nation of Israel (the Jews) but also for all other nations (the Gentiles).

The Wise Men were Gentiles, people not of Abraham's nation. Yet when Jesus the Promised Messiah was born, God sent them a special birth announcement too. He sent angels to the shepherds; He sent a star to the Wise Men.

They saw the star, and they followed. And they followed, and they followed, and they followed. God gave them the faith to believe that the newborn "King of the Jews" was to be a blessing for them as well.

Years later Jesus said to Simon Peter and Andrew, "Follow Me." And they followed. Jesus called to James and John, "Follow Me." And they followed. In following Jesus, they were blessed and became a blessing to others.

Jesus calls us, too, to follow Him. He comes to us to bless us and make us a blessing, whether our family connections are Jewish or Gentile. He comes to bless all people with the forgiveness of sins. His Holy Spirit gives us the faith, as He did the Wise Men, to recognize Jesus as our Savior and King. With the Wise Men we follow . . . and follow . . . and worship Him!

Prayer: God, give us the faith to recognize Jesus as our Savior and King. Help us always to follow where You lead us. Help us to worship You with our whole lives. For Jesus' sake, Amen.

To be sung or read:

As with gladness men of old
Did the guiding star behold,
As with joy they hailed its light
Leading onward, beaming bright,
So, most gracious Lord, may we
Evermore be led by Thee.

As with joyful steps they sped,
Savior, to Thy lowly bed,
There to bend the knee before
Thee whom earth and heaven adore,
So may we with willing feet
Ever seek Thy mercy seat.

Holy Jesus, every day
Keep us in the narrow way
And, when earthly things are past,
Bring our ransomed souls at last
Where they need no star to guide,
Where no clouds Thy glory hide.

Bible Readings: Luke 2:25-32; Romans 15:7-13

In addition: Read the Arch Book, *The Happiest Search.*

Herod

TENTH DAY OF CHRISTMAS

> When **Herod** the king heard this, he was troubled. ...An angel of the Lord appeared to Joseph in a dream and said, "Rise, take the Child and His mother, and flee to Egypt . . . for Herod is about to search for the Child to destroy Him." (Matthew 2:3, 13)

Why would a big strong king be afraid of a teeny tiny baby? How could a grown-up powerful man want to murder a newborn child?

It was a case of mistaken identity. Jesus was born to be King—but not the kind of king Herod was. Herod was afraid of getting bumped off his throne. He feared Jesus would take away the power that Herod treasured. He was scared of losing his job and his crown.

Herod wasn't the only one who misunderstood the kind of king Jesus would be. Many of the people of Israel were hoping the Messiah would be a powerful king who would drive out Herod and the Romans.

But years later, when Jesus was on trial, Pilate asked Him, "Are You King of the Jews?" Jesus answered, "My kingship is not of this world." Jesus was born to be king of our hearts and lives, not of our governments.

Herod was afraid of losing his power. But Jesus didn't come to take away power. He came to bring power—the power of His Spirit, the power of faith, the power of forgiveness, the power of healing, the power of peace. Jesus is our Super-Power, King over all kings, Lord over all lords. And He came to share His power with us.

"Don't be scared," He said, "for it is your Father's good pleasure to give you the kingdom" (Luke 12:32).

Prayer: God, thank You for sending Jesus to bring us into Your kingdom. Rule our hearts and lives with Your love forever. Amen.

To be read or sung:

The star proclaims the King is here;
But, Herod, why this senseless fear?
He takes no realms of earth away
Who gives the realms of heavenly day.

The wiser Magi see from far
And follow on His guiding star;
And led by light, to Light they press
And by their gifts their God confess.

All glory, Jesus, be to Thee
For this Thy glad epiphany;
Whom with the Father we adore
And Holy Ghost forevermore.

Bible Readings: Ephesians 1:15-23; Philippians 2:1-11

In addition: Read the Arch Book, *The Most Wonderful King.*

Gifts

ELEVENTH DAY OF CHRISTMAS

. . . they fell down and worshiped Him. Then, opening their treasures, they offered Him **gifts,** gold and frankincense and myrrh. (Matthew 2:11)

Just about everyone knows what the Wise Men gave to Jesus. Their gold, frankincense, and myrrh are perhaps the most famous presents in all history. (Think of all the Christmas cards you received and sent: how many pictured the Wise Men's treasures?)

And treasures they were. The gifts the Wise Men gave were among the most precious things they could have given. Their gold, frankincense, and myrrh showed great honor to Jesus.

But look again at the Wise Men. What was their most precious gift? What did they offer Jesus *before* they even opened their treasures?

We could easily make a long list of presents we can and do give Jesus. The gifts we give each other, the food and clothes we share with the poor, the money we give to church programs, missions and charities, etc., are all gifts for Him. They are good gifts, and much needed.

But look again at our gifts. The most precious gift we can offer Jesus is ourselves. When we worship Jesus as our Lord and Savior, we are honoring Him with the best of all possible treasures. When we offer Him our lives, it's only natural that our gifts of time, talents, money, and serving will be part of our offering.

The gift of ourselves, of our worship, probably won't make history. We won't be famous and get our pictures on Christmas cards next year. But we do have a promise:

"Whoever confesses that Jesus is the Son of God, God abides in him, and he in God" (1 John 5:15). "And this is what He has promised us, eternal life" (1 John 2:25).

Prayer: God, thank You for the gift of Your Son, Jesus. Accept our worship and all our gifts as signs of our love and faith. Amen.

To be read or sung:

To Thee my heart I offer,
O Christ Child sweet and dear,
Upon Thy love relying,
Oh, be Thou ever near!
Take Thou my heart and give me Thine
And let it be forever mine,
O Jesus, holy, undefiled,
My Savior meek and mild.

Let me be Thine forever,
O Christ Child sweet and dear;
Uphold me with Thy mercy,
And be Thou ever near.
From Thee I gladly all receive
And what is mine to Thee I give,
My heart, my soul, and all I own.
Let these be Thine alone.

Bible Readings: Romans 12; Isaiah 58; Amos 5:21-24; Psalm 51:10-17

For You

. . . to **you** is born this day in the city of David a Savior, who is Christ, the Lord. (Luke 2:11)

Today is the last day of Christmas. Tomorrow is Epiphany. It's the day we celebrate the visit of the Wise Men. The name Epiphany means "to show," or "to make clear." By leading the Wise Men to Jesus, God made clear that His love was for all people—for the people of Israel, for Gentiles, for foreigners, and . . .

. . . for me! Epiphany is, for each one of us, a happy "Aha!" "I get it!" "I can see clearly now!" All the promises, all the waiting, all the miracles are for me! By faith we each discover

God kept His promise to Abraham . . . for me.
Mary and Joseph became parents . . . for me.
Jesus was born as a human baby . . . for me.
He lay in a manger in Bethlehem . . . for me.
The angels announced His birth . . . for me.
The shepherds spread the Good News . . . for me.
The star led the way to Jesus . . . for me.
The Wise Men found the new King . . . for me.
Jesus lived and died and lives . . . for me.
He's ruling the world with His love . . . for me.
He comes today by His Spirit . . . for me.
He comes today through His Word . . . for me.
He comes today in His sacraments . . . for me.
He comes today in people . . . for me.
He's waiting to come again in glory . . . for me.

The Savior, who is Christ, is *my* Lord, personally! Oh, happy day! What good news! What great joy! Merry Christmas to us all! Let's celebrate—while we wait.

Prayer: Glory to God in the highest! Amen!

To be sung or read:

Joy to the world, the Lord is come!
Let earth receive her King;
Let every heart prepare Him room
And heaven and nature sing,
And heaven and nature sing,
And heaven and heaven and nature sing.

Joy to the earth, the Savior reigns!
Let men their songs employ,
While fields and floods, rocks, hills,
    and plains
Repeat the sounding joy,
Repeat the sounding joy,
Repeat, repeat the sounding joy.

He rules the world in truth and grace,
And makes the nations prove
The glories of His righteousness
And wonders of His love,
And wonders of His love,
And wonders, wonders of His love.

Bible Readings: Isaiah 42:5-7; Philippians 4:4-7; Revelation 22:20-21

In addition: Read the Arch Book, *The Innkeeper's Daughter.*

Appendix A

Advent Log

Procure a log at least 6 feet long and 4 inches in diameter, preferably with the bark intact. If necessary plane one side and/or add inconspicuous bracings to stabilize the log and prevent it from rolling over when the candles are in place.

Using a ¾″ bit, drill 28 holes about ¾″ deep at equal intervals in a straight row along the top side of the log.

Determine how many days there are in Advent this year (see "Notes" at front of book) and place that many candles into the log, omitting the farthest holes on both ends as necessary. The candles should be 15 or 18 inches tall in order to provide approximately 20 minutes of candlelight each day. The traditional color for the candles is violet; blue is an alternate choice. Our family uses violet candles for weekdays and white for Sundays in order to emphasize the Easter nature of Sundays, which we feel deserves precedence over the penitential nature of the Advent season as a whole.

When lighting an additional candle each day, follow the alternating ends-to-middle pattern indicated below. Thus the Christmas Eve candle will be the apex of a pyramid of lights.

```
1   3   5   7   9   11  13  15  17  19  21  23  25  27  28  26  24  22  20  18  16  14  12  10  8   6   4   2
```

Decorate the log with branches of evergreens and/or holly sprigs.

Advent Wreath

An Advent wreath is a wreath of evergreens with four candles; one for each week of Advent.

It can be as simple as four free-standing candleholders set in a square on your table and ringed with sprigs of evergreens. It can be as elaborate as a liturgically decorated, wrought-iron frame suspended by a chain from your ceiling and wrapped in garlands of greens and holly.

Many variations of ready-made Advent wreaths are available from religious bookstores and liturgical supply houses. Perhaps the easiest homemade variety is a ring of styrofoam with four candles pressed into it and greens tacked on with straight pins.

Light one candle the first week, two candles the second week, three candles the third week, and all four candles the fourth week. Some Advent wreaths provide a central white candle, a "Christ candle," to light on Christmas Day.

Appendix B

People-ornaments are simply made by pinning photographs to pieces of styrofoam and decorating the remaining exposed surfaces of styrofoam with materials of your choice.

Use various sizes of styrofoam balls sliced in half, and pin the pictures to the flat surfaces. Or use flat sheets of styrofoam cut into squares, triangles, circles, etc., and pin pictures to both front and back flat surfaces (for two-sided ornament).

Frame the picture by pinning metallic braid, tinsel trims, ric-rac, or sequins around its edges. Use short straight pins (sequin pins), and dip the tip of each pin in white glue before putting it into place.

Coat any remaining exposed surfaces of styrofoam with white glue (be careful not to let it drip onto the photograph!) and sprinkle with glitter.

When the ornament is dry, press the ends of a U-shaped wire (the rounded ends of paper clips or hairpins work well, first dipped in glue) into the top of the ornament to provide the loop through which an ornament hook can be slipped.

Appendix C

Advent cookies recipe

Cream together until fluffy:
   1 cup butter or margarine
   2 cups sugar
   3 eggs

Combine and add to above ingredients:
   4 cups flour
   ½ teaspoon salt
   ½ teaspoon baking soda

Divide dough and wrap in 3 or 4 parcels; chill at least 6 hours. Roll and cut dough into Advent symbols by tracing around the cut-out patterns (p. 63) with a paring knife. Place cookies on ungreased cookie sheets and sprinkle lightly with sugar.

Bake at 350° approximately 5—7 minutes or until cookies are lightly browned around edges. (Baking time will vary with thickness and shape of cookies.)

Appendix D

List of correlated Arch Books for suggested supplementary reading:

Day	Title	Day	Title
Advent 6	The Great Promise	Christmas 5	The Baby Born in a Stable
Advent 15	Noah's Ark	Christmas 6	The Night the Angels Sang
Advent 16	The Great Escape	Christmas 8	The Secret of the Star
Advent 17	Mary's Story	Christmas 9	The Happiest Search
(Christmas 2)	(reread Mary's Story)	Christmas 10	The Most Wonderful King
Christmas 4	Little Benjamin and the First Christmas	Christmas 12	The Innkeeper's Daughter

The King of Glory

Willard F. Jabusch

Israeli folksong

Refrain

The King of glo - ry comes, the na - tion re - joic - es;

O - pen the gates be - fore Him, lift up your voic - es.

Stanzas

1 Who is the King of glo - ry; how shall we call Him?
2 In all of Gal - i - lee in cit - y or vil - lage,
3 Sing then of Da - vid's Son, our Sav - ior and Broth - er;
4 He gave His life for us, the Lamb of sal - va - tion,
5 He con - quered sin and death, He tru - ly has ris - en,

1 He is Em - man - u - el, the Prom - ised of a - ges.
2 He goes a - mong His peo - ple cur - ing their ill - ness.
3 In all of Gal - i - lee was nev - er an - oth - er.
4 He took up - on Him - self the sins of the na - tion.
5 And He will share with us His heav - en - ly vi - sion.

God Promised

Words and Music by Linda Schroeder

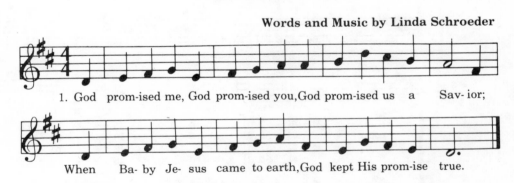

1. God prom-ised me, God prom-ised you, God prom-ised us a Sav-ior;

When Ba- by Je- sus came to earth, God kept His prom-ise true.

2. He came for me. He came for you. He came to be our Savior;
   When Jesus lived like one of us, God kept His promise true.

3. He died for me. He died for you. He died to be our Savior;
   When Jesus died upon the cross, God kept His promise true.

4. He rose again for me and you. He rose to be our Savior;
   When Jesus came to life again, God kept His promise true.

5. He lives today in me and you. He lives to be our Savior;
   When Jesus lives within our hearts, God keeps His promise true.

61

O, Come, O, Come, Emmanuel

Is. 59 : 20
Veni, veni, Emmanuel
Latin author unknown, c. 1100
Tr., John M. Neale, 1851, 1859, ab.

Veni, Emmanuel
Plain-song melody, c. 1200

1 O , come, O , come, Em-man - u - el, And ran-som cap-tive Is - - ra - el That mourns in lone-ly ex - - ile here Un-til the Son of God ap-pear. Re - joice! Re - joice! Em-man - u - el Shall come to thee, O Is - - ra - el.

2 O , come, Thou Rod of Jes - - se, free Thine own from Sa-tan's tyr - an-ny; From depths of hell Thy peo - ple save And give them vic - t'ry o'er the grave. Re - joice! Re - joice! Em-man - u - el Shall come to thee, O Is - - ra - el.

3 O , come, Thou Day-spring from on high, And cheer us by Thy draw-ing nigh; Dis - perse the gloom-y clouds of night And death's dark shad-ows put to flight. Re - joice! Re - joice! Em-man - u - el Shall come to thee, O Is - - ra - el.

4 O , come, Thou Key of Da - - vid, come And o - pen wide our heav'n - ly home; Make safe the way that leads on high And close the path to mis - er - y. Re - joice! Re - joice! Em-man - u - el Shall come to thee, O Is - - ra - el. A-men.